MAKE AND COOK AND BAKE

Elizabeth Eaton

Mills & Boon Limited
London Toronto Sydney

Owlet books are published by Mills & Boon Limited. First published in Great Britain 1975 by Mills & Boon Limited, 17-19 Foley Street, London W1A 1DR.

© Elizabeth Eaton 1975

All rights reserved. No part of this publication may be reproduced, stored in a retrieval system, or transmitted in any form or by any means, electronic, mechanical, photocopying, recording or otherwise, without the prior permission of Mills & Boon.

ISBN 0 263 05934 0

CONTENTS

Introduction 5
Remember 6
Measurements 7
Home-made Sweets
    Chocolate Truffles 8
    Stuffed Dates 10
Biscuits
    Flapjacks 12
    Oat Crunchies 14
    Gingerbread Men 16
    Easter Biscuits 18
Cakes and Scones
    Scones 20
    Cherry Cakes 22
    Victoria Sandwich 24
    Rock Cakes 26
    Chocolate Butterfly Cakes 28
    Butter Icing 31
Pastry
    Sausage Rolls 32
    Apple Dumplings 34
    Jam Tarts 36
    Bread Rolls 38
Simple Main Meals
    Cheese Salad 40
    Poached Egg on Toast 42
Cold Sweets
    Gooseberry Fool 44
    Peach Melba 46

INTRODUCTION

Have you ever helped your mother with cooking in the kitchen? It is great fun making your own little pie with the leftover scraps of pastry. Of course, it's much better to have your own recipe book. I have collected some easy recipes and put them all together for you. Some of you will have already used the first **Make and Play** cookery book, *You Can Cook, It's Fun!*, which is a little easier than this one.

Always ask your mother first before you start cooking. She will then be ready to help you with any difficult or dangerous tasks.

Before you start to cook, read my list under the heading 'Remember'. To enjoy cookery, there are some things you must never forget.

REMEMBER

1. Always wash your hands, taking care to scrub your nails.
2. Put on an apron.
3. Wipe the table top.
4. Read the recipe first.
5. Put out all the ingredients and utensils before starting to cook.
6. If you are using the oven, ask your mother to turn it on. It takes up to 10 minutes to heat up.
7. Never leave saucepan handles sticking out on the top of the cooker.
8. Wash up afterwards and leave the kitchen clean and tidy.
9. Never touch anything hot. Always use oven gloves.
10. When you use a knife, always cut away from your fingers.
11. Always ask your mother if you have a problem.

MEASUREMENTS

Here are some measurements used in this book that you will need to know.

teasp – teaspoon
Tbs – tablespoon
g – gram
oz – ounce
lb – pound
ml – millilitre
pt – pint
C – Celsius
F – Fahrenheit
mm – millimetre
cm – centimetre
" – inch

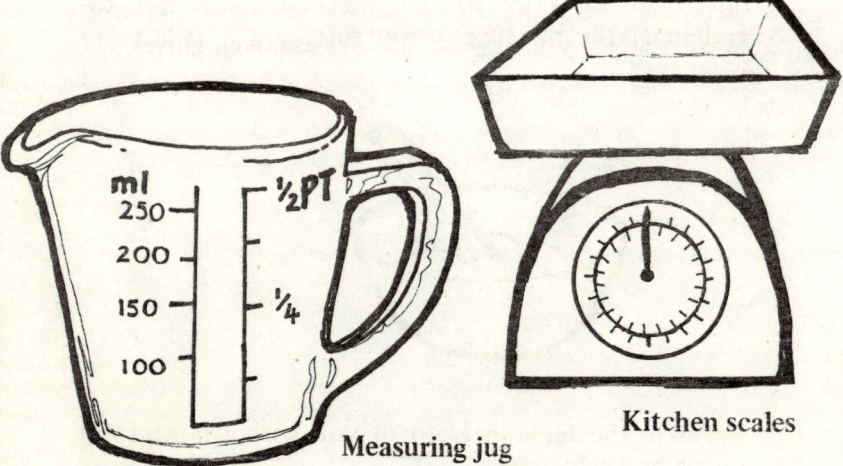

Set of measuring spoons

Measuring jug

Kitchen scales

Some of the cookery books your mother uses have the old method of measuring pounds and ounces. I have included these in the book for your mother's benefit. It would be too difficult to be exact all the time with the conversions from ounces to grams, so they are rounded off to make measuring easier.

HOME-MADE SWEETS

Chocolate Truffles

100 g (4 oz) margarine
2½ Tbs cocoa powder
1½ Tbs icing sugar

1. Wash your hands. Put on an apron.

2. Measure out the softened margarine and cocoa. Place in a mixing bowl.
   Measure the icing sugar and sieve into the mixing bowl.

3. Mix all the ingredients together with a wooden spoon until the mixture becomes creamy. You may add a few drops of water to help the ingredients mix together. If the mixture is too soft, add a little more icing sugar.

4. Sprinkle the table in front of you with a mixture of cocoa and icing sugar.

Take a teaspoonful of the mixture from the bowl. Work it into a ball. Roll it in the cocoa and sugar.

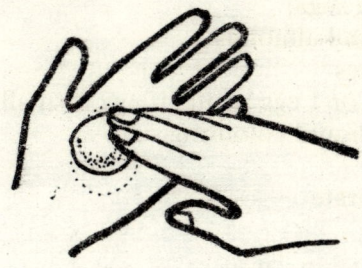

5   When you have used up the mixture in the bowl, place the chocolate truffles on a plate to harden.

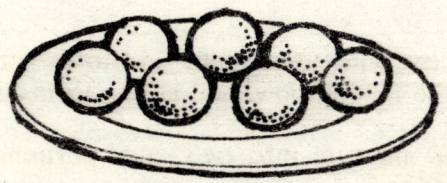

Stuffed Dates

50 g (2 oz) icing sugar
50 g (2 oz) ground almonds
200 g (8 oz) dates
½ an egg white, or 1 egg white, if egg is small
Pink and green liquid colouring
Silver balls
Walnuts to decorate

1   Wash your hands. Put on an apron.

2   Sieve the icing sugar and add to the ground almonds in a mixing bowl.
Separate the egg yolk from the egg white. Pour it through a straining spoon into a small bowl.

3   Beat the egg white. Gradually add to the dry ingredients in the mixing bowl and stir to form a soft, firm paste.
Divide the mixture into two equal portions and put one half aside.

4   Put one drop of green colouring on a teaspoon, then add it to the paste in the bowl. Mix well.

Turn out the paste on to a sugared board. Knead lightly until it is smooth.
Now put one drop of pink colouring on a teaspoon, then add it to the rest of the paste in another bowl. Mix well, then turn out the paste on to the sugared board and knead it lightly.

5 Remove the stones from the dates with the end of a knife. Keep your fingers away from the blade.
Make the almond paste into sausage shapes. Place one sausage shape inside each date.

6 Decorate the dates with silver balls and small pieces of walnuts.
Place the dates on a plate.

BISCUITS
Flapjacks

150 g (6 oz) margarine
150 g (6 oz) demerara sugar
200 g (8 oz) quick-cooking rolled oats
2 Tbs golden syrup
Pinch of salt
¼ teasp mixed spice
6 walnuts

1. Wash your hands. Put on an apron.
   Turn on the oven, gas mark 4, or 350°F (180°C). Take a shallow baking tray, approximately 30 cm x 20 cm (12" x 8"), and rub all over the inside with a small piece of lard.

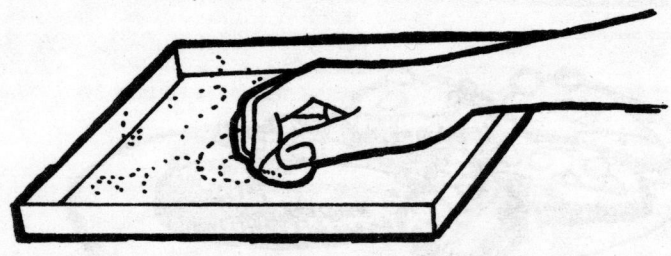

2. Put the sugar, rolled oats, salt and mixed spice into a mixing bowl.
   Chop a few walnuts into little pieces and put them in the mixing bowl.

3. Melt the margarine and syrup in a saucepan over a low heat. Remove from the heat.
   Pour the melted margarine and syrup over the dry ingredients.

4   Stir the mixture well. Put it all into the well-greased tray and press down firmly.
    Place the tray in the oven using oven gloves. Bake for 30-35 minutes. When the contents are golden brown, remove the tray from the oven with oven gloves.

5   Cut into fingers while mixture is still in the tray. Allow to cool completely, then ease out fingers with a palette knife.

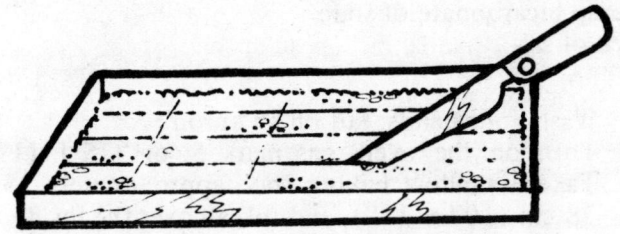

Place the flapjacks on a plate.

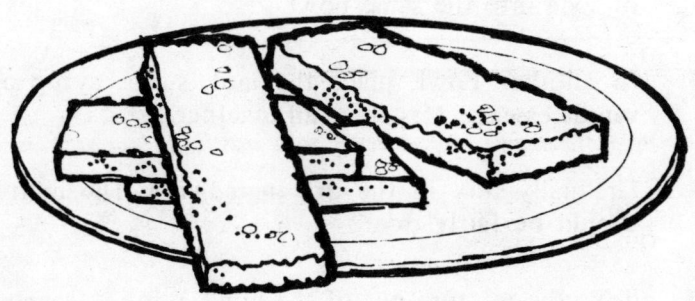

Oat Crunchies

100 g (4 oz) plain flour
100 g (4 oz) lard
75 g (3 oz) sugar
100 g (4 oz) porridge oats
1 teasp baking powder
2 teasp golden syrup
½ teasp vanilla essence
½ teasp bicarbonate of soda
Pinch of salt

1. Wash your hands. Put on an apron.
   Turn on the oven, gas mark 5, or 375°F (190°C). Take a shallow baking tray, approximately 25 cm x 28 cm (10" x 11"), and rub all over the inside with a small piece of lard.

2. Put the porridge oats in a mixing bowl.
   Sieve the flour, salt, baking powder and bicarbonate of soda into the same bowl.

3. In another bowl, place the lard, sugar, syrup and vanilla essence. Mix them all together.

4. Gradually mix in the dry ingredients. The mixture should be fairly dry.

5. Take the mixture out of the bowl, using a teaspoon. Roll it into small balls, with a little flour if necessary. Put the balls on the baking tray and flatten them slightly.

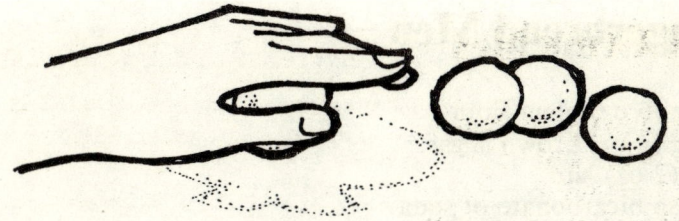

6. Using oven gloves, place the tray in the oven and bake for 10-15 minutes. When the biscuits are light brown, remove the tray from the oven, using oven gloves. Allow to cool, then place the oat crunchies on a plate with a palette knife.

Gingerbread Men

150 g (6 oz) plain flour
100 g (4 oz) brown sugar
50 g (2 oz) lard
1 teasp bicarbonate of soda
1 teasp ground ginger
1½ Tbs golden syrup
1 egg
Pinch of salt
Sultanas for eyes
Cherries for mouth

1. Wash your hands. Put on an apron.
   Turn on the oven, gas mark 5, or 375°F (190°C). Take a shallow baking tray, approximately 30 cm x 20 cm (12" x 8"). Rub all over the inside with a small piece of lard.

2. Sieve the flour into a mixing bowl.
   Put the salt, ginger, bicarbonate of soda and sugar into the same bowl.

3. Put the lard and golden syrup in a saucepan. Melt them over a low heat on top of the cooker. When they are completely melted, turn off the heat and remove the saucepan from the cooker.
   Pour this melted mixture over the dry ingredients in the mixing bowl.

4. Stir well until cool.
   Add the egg and stir well again. The mixture will now be sticky.

5   Sprinkle flour on to the pastry board in front of you. Remove the mixture from the bowl with a wooden spoon. With the help of a little flour, roll out the mixture on the pastry board, using a rolling pin. Roll the mixture until it is 6 mm (¼") thick all over.

6   Use a gingerbread-man cutter to cut out the shapes. Or cut out the legs, arms, heads and bodies with a knife. Join up the parts of the body, pressing them together firmly with a little water.
Use sultanas for eyes and slices of cherries for mouth.

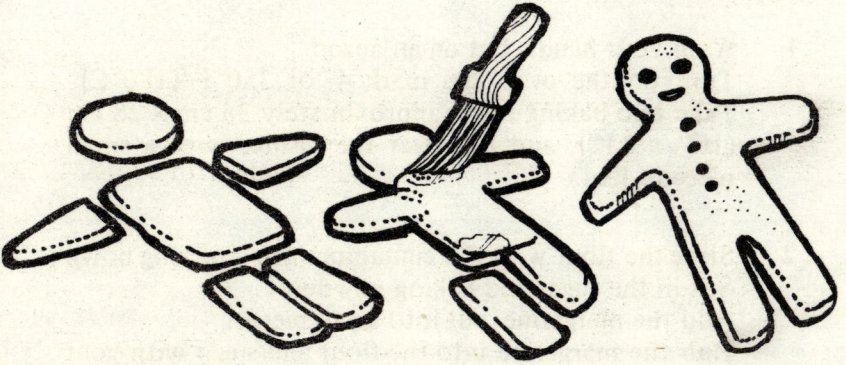

Place them on the greased tray and put the tray in the oven using oven gloves. Bake for 20 minutes. When they are golden brown, remove the tray from the oven with oven gloves.
Allow to cool, then place the gingerbread men on a plate with a palette knife.

Easter Biscuits

200 g (8 oz) plain flour
100 g (4 oz) margarine
100 g (4 oz) caster sugar
50 g (2 oz) currants
½ teasp baking powder
1 egg
½ teasp ground cinnamon
Milk if necessary

1   Wash your hands. Put on an apron.
    Turn on the oven, gas mark 4, or 350°F (180°C).
    Take two baking trays, approximately 25 cm x 28 cm (10" x 11"), and rub over the insides with a small piece of lard.

2   Sieve the flour with the cinnamon into a mixing bowl.
    Stir in the sugar and baking powder.
    Add the margarine, cut into small pieces.
    Rub the margarine into the flour and sugar with your fingers, until the mixture looks like breadcrumbs.

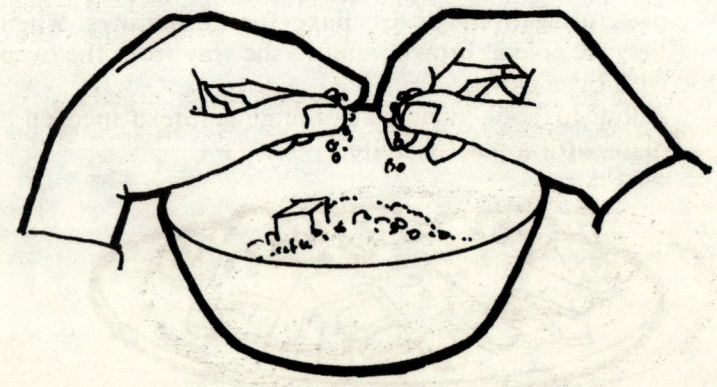

3   Stir in the currants.
    Beat the egg in a cup with a fork. Stir the egg into the mixture.
    Mix to a stiff dough, using a little milk if it is too dry.
    Put the mixture on a floured pastry board.

4   Roll out the dough, using a little flour if it is sticky, until it is 6 mm (¼″) thick all over.
    Cut it into biscuits with a pastry cutter and place these on the baking trays.

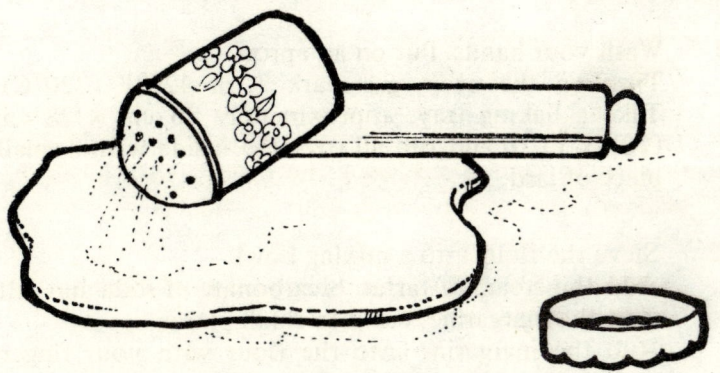

5   Using oven gloves, place the trays in the oven and bake for 20-30 minutes. When the biscuits are light brown, remove the trays from the oven, using oven gloves.
    Allow to cool, then place the biscuits on a plate with a palette knife.

CAKES AND SCONES

Scones

100 g (4 oz) plain flour
25 g (1 oz) margarine
25 g (1 oz) sultanas
25 g (1 oz) sugar
½ teasp cream of tartar
¼ teasp bicarbonate of soda
¼ teasp salt
50 ml ($\frac{1}{8}$ pt) milk

1 Wash your hands. Put on an apron.
 Turn on the oven, gas mark 7, or 425°F (220°C). Take a baking tray, approximately 25 cm x 28 cm (10" x 11"), and rub all over the inside with a small piece of lard.

2 Sieve the flour into a mixing bowl.
 Add the cream of tartar, bicarbonate of soda and salt.
 Add the margarine, cut into small pieces.
 Rub the margarine into the flour with your fingers until it looks like breadcrumbs.

3 Stir in the sultanas and sugar.
 Pour in the milk, a little at a time, leaving some to brush the scones.
 Mix to a soft dough.
 Knead the mixture into a ball. Put it on a floured pastry board.

4 Roll it out carefully until it is 1 cm (½") thick all over. Sprinkle flour over the dough if it is sticky. Cut into rounds with a pastry cutter. Place these on the baking tray.

Brush the scones with a little milk to help them brown.

5   Using oven gloves, place the tray in the oven and bake for 10-12 minutes. When the scones are golden brown, remove the tray from the oven, again using oven gloves.
Allow to cool, then place the scones on a plate with a palette knife.

Cherry Cakes

100 g (4 oz) margarine
100 g (4 oz) sugar
100 g (4 oz) self-raising flour
2 eggs
1 Tbs warm water
Glacé cherries

1   Wash your hands. Put on an apron.
    Turn on the oven, gas mark 4, or 350°F (180°C).
    Place some paper cake cases in a 12-hole bun tin.

2   Place the margarine and sugar in a bowl. Beat together until light and creamy.
    Break the eggs into a cup.

3   Add the eggs to the mixture slowly. Beat well.
    Add the warm water.

4   Add the sifted flour. Stir well until it is all mixed together.
    Now stir in some chopped cherries.

5   Put a tablespoonful of mixture into each paper case.

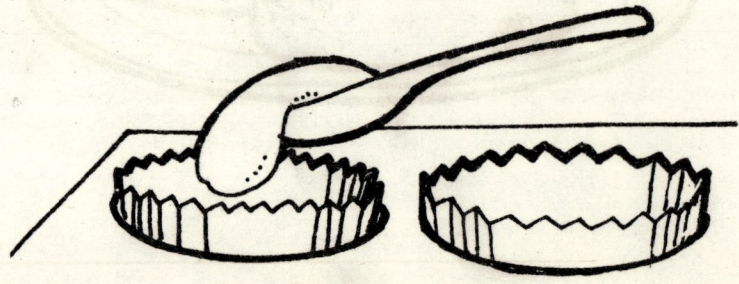

Place half a cherry on top of each cake.
Put the tin in the oven using oven gloves. Bake for 20 minutes.

6   When the cherry cakes are golden brown, remove the tray from the oven using oven gloves.
Leave to cool.
Place the cakes on a plate.

Victoria Sandwich

100 g (4 oz) margarine
100 g (4 oz) caster sugar
100 g (4 oz) plain flour
2 eggs
1 Tbs warm water
1 teasp baking powder
Jam for filling
Icing sugar to decorate

1   Wash your hands. Put on an apron.
    Turn on the oven, gas mark 4, or 350°F (180°C).
    Take two 15 cm (6") sandwich cake tins and rub all over the inside with a small piece of lard.

2   Beat the margarine and sugar in a mixing bowl, using a wooden spoon, until they are light and creamy. Beat the eggs in a basin. Add the eggs to the mixture, a little at a time, and beat well. Then add the warm water.

3   Sieve the flour and baking powder into a bowl.
    Stir the flour and baking powder slowly into the cake mixture.

4   Divide the mixture between the two cake tins.

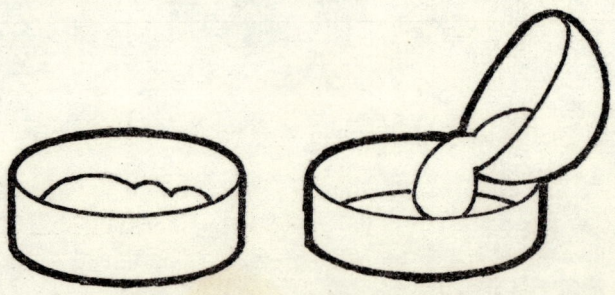

Using oven gloves, place the tins in the oven and bake for 30 minutes.

5   Ask an adult to help you test the cake. When it is firm and light brown on top, it is ready to be taken out of the oven. Use oven gloves.
Tip the cakes out of the tins on to a wire tray. Leave to cool.

6   To decorate, spread jam between the two layers of cake. Press these layers together. Sprinkle icing sugar on top of the cake.
Place the Victoria sandwich on a plate.

Rock Cakes

200 g (8 oz) self-raising flour
100 g (4 oz) margarine
100 g (4 oz) sugar
75 g (3 oz) currants
25 g (1 oz) chopped candied peel
½ teasp mixed spice
Pinch of salt
1 egg
A little milk if necessary

1 Wash your hands. Put on an apron.
  Turn on the oven, gas mark 6, or 400°F (200°C).
  Take two baking trays, approximately 25 cm x 28 cm (10" x 11"), and rub all over the insides with a small piece of lard.

2 Sieve the flour and salt into a mixing bowl.
  Add the mixed spice.

3   Add the margarine, cut into small pieces.
    Rub the margarine into the flour, until it looks like fine breadcrumbs.
    Stir in the sugar, currants and candied peel, using a fork.

4   Beat the egg in a basin. Add to dry ingredients using a fork.
    Mix all the ingredients very well until the mixture is fairly firm and dry. You may need to add a drop of milk.

5   Using a fork or spoon, put the mixture in small heaps on the baking trays.
    Put the baking trays in the oven using oven gloves.
    Bake for 15 minutes.

6   When the rock cakes are golden brown, remove them from the oven, using oven gloves.
    Take the cakes off the trays, using a palette knife, and leave to cool on a wire tray.
    Place the cakes on a plate.

Chocolate Butterfly Cakes

100 g (4 oz) self-raising flour
100 g (4 oz) margarine
100 g (4 oz) sugar
2 eggs
25 g (1 oz) cocoa powder
¼ teasp vanilla essence
½ Tbs golden syrup

1   Wash your hands. Put on an apron.
Turn on the oven, gas mark 5, or 375°F (190°C).
Take a 12-hole bun tin and place a paper cake case in each hole.

2   Beat the margarine and sugar together in a bowl, until they are light and creamy. This is called creaming.
Beat in the eggs one at a time.
Mix thoroughly, adding the golden syrup and vanilla essence.

3   Sieve the flour and cocoa powder into a bowl.
    Stir the dry ingredients into the creamed mixture until it is quite soft.

4   Half fill each paper case with the mixture.
    Put the tin in the oven, using oven gloves. Bake for 15-20 minutes.

5   When the cakes are firm, take them out of the oven with oven gloves.
    Place the buns on a wire tray to cool.

6   When the cakes are cold, remove the paper cases, and cut off the top of each cake.
    Divide each top in half for the 'wings'.

7   Put a teaspoonful of butter icing (see page 31) on each cake. Place the wings on top.
Put all the butterfly cakes on a plate.

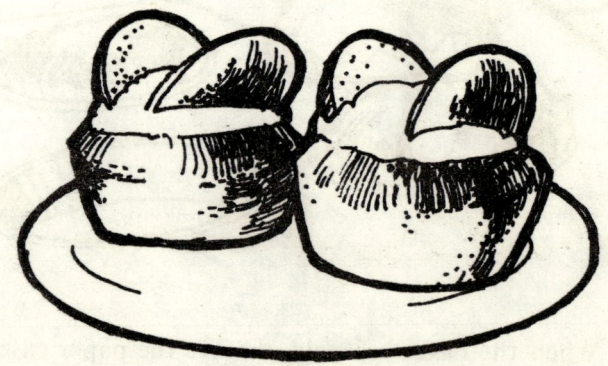

Butter Icing

75 g (3 oz) icing sugar
50 g (2 oz) butter or margarine
1 teasp warm water
Vanilla essence

1   Sieve the icing sugar into a mixing bowl.
    Add the margarine and stir well with a wooden spoon, until the mixture is soft and creamy.
    Add 3 drops of vanilla essence, using a teaspoon. Add a little warm water if the mixture is too stiff.
    Stir well.

PASTRY

Sausage Rolls

200 g (8 oz) plain flour
100 g (4 oz) lard
Pinch of salt
Cold water to mix
} Shortcrust pastry

200 g (8 oz) sausages
A little milk

1. Wash your hands. Put on an apron.
   Turn on the oven, gas mark 7, or 425°F (220°C).
   Get out two baking trays, approximately 25 cm x 28 cm (10" x 11").
   Take the skins off the sausages using a pair of scissors.

2. Sieve the flour and salt into a mixing bowl.
   Add the lard, chopped into small pieces.
   Rub the mixture together with your fingers until it looks like fine breadcrumbs. Mix in enough water to moisten the mixture.
   Collect it all together in one big ball.

3. Divide the mixture in half.
   Roll out one half of the pastry into an oblong shape on a floured board. Trim the edges straight with a knife.
   Place half the sausages along one long straight edge of the pastry.

4   Roll the pastry up. Stick the edges together with water.
    Brush the top with milk. This helps the pastry turn golden brown.
    Cut this long roll into small sausage rolls. With a knife make two little cuts on the top of each roll.
    Place the rolls on the baking trays.
    Repeat with the rest of the pastry and the sausages.

5   Using oven gloves, place the trays in the oven and bake for 25 minutes.
    When the rolls are golden brown, remove them from the oven, using oven gloves.
    Lift the rolls off the trays with a palette knife. Leave to cool on a wire tray.
    Place them on a plate. Sausage rolls are usually eaten hot.

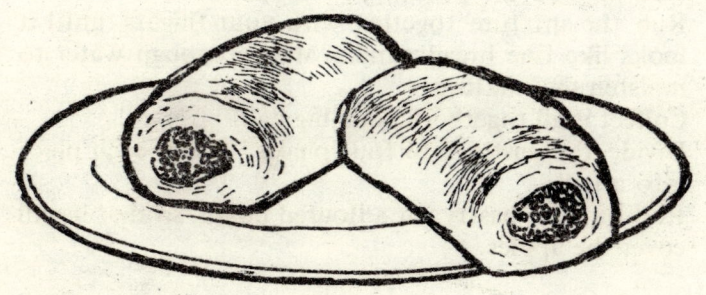

Apple Dumplings

150 g (6 oz) plain flour
75 g (3 oz) lard
Pinch of salt
Cold water to mix
} Shortcrust pastry

50 g (2 oz) stoned dates
4 cooking apples
4 teasp brown sugar

1. Wash your hands. Put on an apron.
   Turn on the oven, gas mark 6, or 400°F (200°C). Get out a baking tray, approximately 25 cm x 28 cm (10" x 11").

2. Peel the apples. Remove all the core by scooping out with the apple peeler.

3. Sieve the flour and salt into a mixing bowl.
   Add the lard, chopped into small pieces.
   Rub the mixture together with your fingers, until it looks like fine breadcrumbs. Mix in enough water to moisten the mixture.
   Collect it all together in one big ball.
   Divide the pastry into four pieces. Knead each piece into a ball.
   Roll out the pastry on a floured board, so that it will cover the apples.

4. Cut the stoned dates into small pieces.
   Fill up the centres of the apples with the stoned dates and a teaspoonful of brown sugar in each apple.

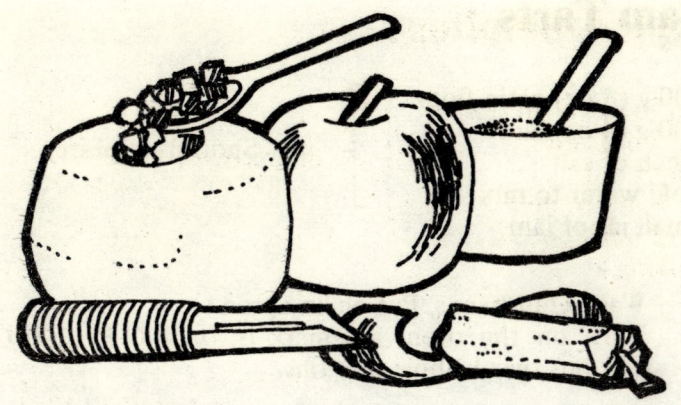

Stand each apple on a round of pastry. Wrap the pastry round the apples and smooth down the edges, using a little cold water.

5 Turn the apples upside down and put them on the baking tray.
Using oven gloves, place the tray in the oven and bake for 30 minutes.
When the dumplings are light brown, remove the tray, using oven gloves.

6 Apple dumplings are usually eaten hot with custard or cream. They can also be eaten cold.

Jam Tarts

200 g (8 oz) plain flour
100 g (4 oz) lard
Pinch of salt
Cold water to mix
Small jar of jam

⎤ Shortcrust pastry

1   Wash your hands. Put on an apron.
    Turn on the oven, gas mark 6, or 400°F (200°C).
    Get out two 12-hole bun tins.

2   Sieve the flour and salt into a mixing bowl.
    Add the lard, chopped into small pieces.
    Rub the mixture together with your fingers, until it looks like fine breadcrumbs. Mix in enough water to moisten the mixture.
    Collect it all together in one big ball.
    Roll out the pastry on a floured board until it is about 6 mm (¼″) thick all over.
    Use a small, round pastry cutter to cut out as many shapes as possible.

Place the rounds of pastry in the two bun tins.

3 Put a teaspoonful of jam into each pastry case.

Using oven gloves, place the tins in the oven and bake for 15-20 minutes.

4 When the tarts are cooked, remove the tins from the oven, using oven gloves.
Ease tarts out with the point of a knife and leave to cool on a wire tray.
Place the tarts on a plate.

Bread Rolls

200 g (8 oz) plain flour
25 g (1 oz) lard
2 teasp baking powder
125 ml (¼ pt) milk
1 egg
Pinch of salt

1   Wash your hands. Put on an apron.
    Turn on the oven, gas mark 6, or 400°F (200°C). Take a baking tray, approximately 25 cm x 28 cm (10" x 11"), and rub all over the inside with a small piece of lard.

2   Sieve the flour and the baking powder into a mixing bowl.
    Add the salt.
    Add the lard, chopped into small pieces.
    Rub the mixture together with your fingers.

3   Add the egg and a little of the milk. Mix well to make a dough. Add more milk if necessary.

4   With the help of a little flour, knead the dough lightly and form it into small rolls.
    Place the rolls on the tray. Brush each roll with a little milk.

5   Using oven gloves, place the tray in the oven and bake for 15 minutes.
    When the rolls are firm and golden brown, remove the tray from the oven with oven gloves.
    Put the rolls on a wire tray to cool. Do not cut them until they are cold.

6   Serve them with butter and jam.

SIMPLE MAIN MEALS

Cheese Salad

1 lettuce
2 eggs
A few spring onions
A few radishes
2 tomatoes
¼ cucumber
100 g (4 oz) cheese

1   Wash your hands. Put on an apron.

2   Remove the outer leaves of the lettuce and wash the rest under running water. Leave to drain.

3   Hard boil 2 eggs by putting them in a saucepan and covering them with cold water. Place the saucepan on the heat and bring to the boil. When the water is boiling, turn down the heat and time the eggs for 10 minutes. Remove the saucepan from the heat and leave the eggs to cool.

4   Cut off the roots and stalks of the radishes. Wash and leave to drain.
    Cut off the roots and tops of the stalks of the spring onions. Remove the skin. The onions can be served sliced or whole.

5   Wipe the tomatoes and slice them.
    Wipe the cucumber and slice it.
    Always use a cutting board. Hold the knife firmly and cut downwards, keeping your fingers away from the blade.

6   Grate the cheese.
    When the eggs are cool, take the shells off and slice them carefully.

7   Place the lettuce leaves on two dinner plates. Arrange the other ingredients on top, with the cheese piled in the centre.

Poached Egg on Toast

2 eggs
2 slices of bread
Butter

1 Wash your hands. Put on an apron.

2 Put some water in the base of the egg poacher and bring to the boil.
   Melt a little butter in 2 of the poaching cups.

3 First break one egg into a cup, then put it into the poaching cup.
   Do the same with the second egg.
   Cover with a lid and simmer for 3-4 minutes.

4   Prepare some toast by putting two slices of bread in an electric toaster. Or put the bread under the grill until the bread is golden brown on both sides.
Butter the toast.
Use a palette knife to remove the eggs from the poacher. Place the eggs on top of the toast.
Serve the eggs and toast on warm plates.

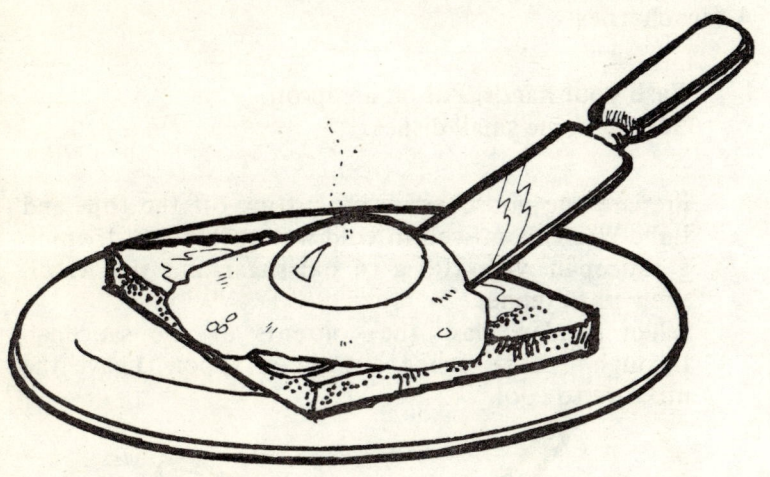

COLD SWEETS

Gooseberry Fool

400 g (1 lb) gooseberries
125 g (5 oz) sugar
125 ml (¼ pt) water
250 ml (½ pt) milk
15 g (½ oz) custard powder
1 Tbs single cream, if available
A few cherries

1. Wash your hands. Put on an apron. Get out some small dishes.

2. Prepare the gooseberries by cutting off the tops and tails. Wash them well in cold water, then put them in a saucepan with 100 g (4 oz) sugar and the water. Stew until tender.
   When tender, pass the contents of the saucepan through a sieve, using a wooden spoon. Leave the mixture to cool.

3. Put the custard powder in a bowl with the remaining sugar and 2 Tbs of cold milk. Stir until the mixture is smooth and creamy.

4 Put the rest of the milk in a saucepan and bring to the boil. When boiled, turn off the heat and pour the milk over the custard mixture. Stir, then return the mixture to the saucepan and reheat.
Stir constantly until it thickens. Remove from the heat after 3 minutes. Leave to cool.

5 Whisk the custard and the cream into the gooseberry mixture.
Pour the gooseberry fool into individual dishes. Decorate with cherries.

Peach Melba

1 small tin of halved peaches
2 Tbs raspberry jam
125 ml (¼ pt) double cream, if available
1 block of vanilla ice cream
6 wafer biscuits

1   Wash your hands. Put on an apron.
     Get out three small dishes.

2   Open the tin of peaches using a tin opener. Remove the peaches and leave to drain.
     Put the jam into a sieve with a tablespoon of peach syrup. Sieve into a bowl to make the Melba sauce.

3   Whip up the cream in a bowl with a whisk until it is fairly stiff.

4   Put a spoonful of ice cream in each dish.

5   Put 2 peach halves in each dish. Arrange them on either side of the ice cream.

6   Put a spoonful of Melba sauce on top of the ice cream. Decorate with some cream and serve with wafers.

INDEX OF RECIPES

Apple dumplings	34
Bread rolls	38
Butter icing	31
Cheese salad	40
Cherry cakes	22
Chocolate butterfly cakes	28
Chocolate truffles	8
Easter biscuits	18
Flapjacks	12
Gingerbread men	16
Gooseberry fool	44
Jam tarts	36
Oat crunchies	14
Peach Melba	46
Poached egg on toast	42
Rock cakes	26
Sausage rolls	32
Scones	20
Stuffed dates	10
Victoria sandwich	24